ALL ABOUT US

Our Dreams, Our World, Our Friendship

WRITTEN BY ELLEN BAILEY

ILLUSTRATED BY NELLIE RYAN

EDITED BY NICOLA BAXTER,
HANNAH DAFFERN, AND
AMANDA LEARMONTH
DESIGNED BY BARBARA WARD
COVER ARTWORK BY NELLIE RYAN
COVER DESIGNED BY ANGIE ALLISON

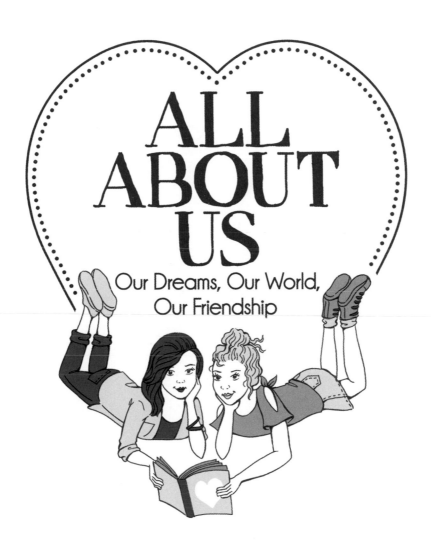

ALL ABOUT US

Our Dreams, Our World, Our Friendship

Andrews McMeel
PUBLISHING®

Andrews McMeel Publishing
a division of Andrews McMeel Universal
1130 Walnut Street, Kansas City, Missouri 64106

www.andrewsmcmeel.com

First published in Great Britain in 2017 by Buster Books, an imprint of Michael O'Mara
Books, Ltd. 9 Lion Yard, Tremadoc Road, London SW4 7NQ

18 19 20 21 22 SHO 10 9 8 7 6 5 4 3 2 1

ISBN: 978-1-4494-9171-0

Library of Congress Control Number: 2017949449

Made by:
Shanghai Offset Printing Products LTD
Address and place of production:
No. 1320, Xinwei, Liguang Community,
Guanlan Subdistrict, Bao an District, Shenzhen,
Guangdong Province, China 518110
1st printing—11/6/17

Editor: Jean Z. Lucas
Art Director: Julie Barnes
Production Manager: Carol Coe
Production Editor: Kevin Kotur

CONTENTS

Let's get started 7

All about us: the fact file 8

Knowing me . . . knowing you . . . 10

Our best moments of ALL time 13

Seeing eye to eye 14

Mystic minds 16

Picture perfect 18

A year of things to do together 24

Things we find SO annoying 26

A problem shared is a problem halved 27

Tiny times 29

Sleep fact file 30

Super sleepover planner 32

Fashion style challenge 34

Choices, choices 39

I wanna be . . . you wanna be . . . 40

And the winner is . . . 45

Fashionista or . . . fashion flop? 50

Happy vacations 52

Trip of a lifetime 54

Face your fears 56

Fabulous feasts 58

Go on, I dare you! 60

Best friend star awards 62

I can . . . can you? 64

Purr-fect pals	66	Birthday wish list	104
Hand in hand	68	Silly sketches	106
Our dream party	70	Memory test	108
I ♡ TV . . . you ♡ TV	72	Which smoothie are you?	110
Signature style	74	Design a fort	112
Name game	78	The future's in your hands	113
Top 10 tunes	80	Bestie band world tour	116
So emoji-onal!	82	BFF book awards	118
Movie match	84	Color us happy	120
Which animal are you?	86	Going for gold	122
That was SO embarrassing!	91	Makeover mates	126
Oodles of doodles	92		
Decisions . . . decisions	98		
Secret codes	99		
Friendship fortune wheel	102		

LET'S GET STARTED

THERE'S NOTHING BETTER THAN SHARING YOUR MOST PRECIOUS THOUGHTS, FEELINGS, AND DREAMS WITH YOUR BEST FRIENDS. INSIDE, YOU'LL FIND LOTS OF WAYS TO RECORD JUST WHAT MAKES YOUR BFFS SO SPECIAL.

Here's how it works. For some activities, you and your best friend each fill in your own page. There's a space at the bottom of the page to show who is filling it in, like this:

This page was completed by ....

Other pages ask you to decide together what to write, and some pages are for you and a group of friends to complete.

You don't have to read this book in any particular order. Just find a page that fits the mood and the moment. Record the time and place when you see spaces like this:

Date .... Time .... Place ....

THIS BOOK IS ALL ABOUT FUN AND FRIENDSHIP— JUST LIKE YOUR BFFS. ENJOY!

ALL ABOUT US:
THE FACT FILE

Fill in the fact file below all about you.

Date   Time   Place

My name is

My nickname is

My birthday is on

The place I was born is called

My star sign is

My hair color is

I have   brothers and   sisters

Right now I'm   years old

Now complete this one for your BFF.

(If you can't complete this for your BFF, just ask her!)

My BFF's name is

Her nickname is

Her birthday is on

The place she was born is called

Her star sign is

Her hair color is

She has   brothers and   sisters

Right now she's   years old

KNOWING ME . . .

HOW WELL DOES YOUR BFF KNOW YOU?
ASK HER TO FILL IN THIS PAGE ABOUT YOU. CHECK HOW
MANY SHE GOT RIGHT, THEN TURN TO PAGE 12 FOR THE VERDICT.

1. What is my full name? ....

2. What is my favorite song? ....

3. What is my dream job? ....

4. Who is my secret crush? ....

5. What is my favorite food? ....

6. What is my favorite color? ....

7. What do I want for my next birthday? ....

8. What am I most scared of? ....

9. What is my favorite lesson? ....

10. Who do I most admire? ....

Score

$\overline{10}$

Date .... Time .... Place ....
This page was completed by ....

10

KNOWING YOU . . .

NOW, HOW WELL DO YOU KNOW YOUR BFF?
FILL IN THIS PAGE ABOUT YOUR BFF. ASK HER HOW
MANY YOU GOT RIGHT, THEN TURN TO PAGE 12 FOR THE VERDICT.

1. What is my full name? ....

2. What is my favorite song? ....

3. What is my dream job? ....

4. Who is my secret crush? ....

5. What is my favorite food? ....

6. What is my favorite color? ....

7. What do I want for my next birthday? ....

8. What am I most scared of? ....

9. What is my favorite lesson? ....

10. Who do I most admire? ....

Score

$$\overline{10}$$

Date .... Time .... Place ....
This page was completed by ....

KNOWING US . . . THE VERDICT

0-3

It might not look as though you are the best of buddies, but you do get along together. Maybe you've been so busy having fun you haven't had time to get to know each other better. This book will certainly help to change that.

4-7

You know your BFF pretty well, but perhaps you could use some quiet time together to really get to know each other and become best buds forever.

8-10

There's no doubt you are super-besties. You have a friendship built to last and you know each other inside out. You are always there for one another, through thick and thin.

OUR BEST MOMENTS
OF ALL TIME

LIST THE FIVE MOST MEMORABLE MOMENTS YOU'VE SHARED,
PERHAPS WHEN YOU HAD YOUR FIRST SLEEPOVER, OR THE
TIME YOU BOTH LAUGHED SO MUCH YOUR SIDES HURT.

1. ....
....

2. ....
....

3. ....
....

4. ....
....

5. ....
....

Date .... Time .... Place ....
This page was completed by .... and ....

13

seeing eye to eye

WITHOUT CHEATING, COMPLETE THE SENTENCE BELOW.

I think my BFF's eye color is: ....

NOW LOOK CLOSELY AT HER EYES. WERE YOU RIGHT?

My BFF's eye color is actually: ....

USING THE PICTURE BELOW, DRAW THE COLORS YOU
CAN SEE IN YOUR BFF'S EYES.

Then add a pair of glasses or sunglasses designed just for her.
Make sure they are as brilliant as she is. . . .

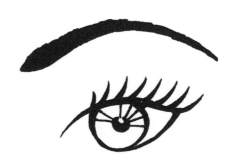

Date .... Time .... Place ....
This page was completed by ....

WITHOUT CHEATING, COMPLETE THE SENTENCE BELOW.

I think my BFF's eye color is: ....

NOW LOOK CLOSELY AT HER EYES. WERE YOU RIGHT?

My BFF's eye color is actually: ....

USING THE PICTURE BELOW, DRAW THE COLORS YOU
CAN SEE IN YOUR BFF'S EYES.

Then add a pair of glasses or sunglasses designed just for her.
Make sure they are as brilliant as she is. . . .

Date .... Time .... Place ....
This page was completed by ....

15

MYSTIC MINDS

HOW IN TUNE are YOU WITH YOUR BFF? SECRETLY WRITE DOWN THE ANSWERS TO THE QUESTIONS BELOW. THEN COVER THEM UP!

1. Write the first color you think of ....

2. Name a film you love ....

3. Think of a girl's name beginning with "S" ....

4. Draw either a square, a circle, or a diamond ....

5. Name a song you like ....

6. Write a number between 1 and 10 ....

7. Name a famous person ....

8. Think of a month of the year ....

WHAT'S YOUR SPOOKY SCORE? 0-4: You may not always think along the same lines, but you can pick up on each other's feelings when it really counts.

Date .... Time .... Place ....

This page was completed by ....

NOW, GET YOUR BFF TO FILL IN HER ANSWERS BELOW SO YOU CAN TAKE A TELEPATHY TEST! COMPARE YOUR ANSWERS AND COUNT ONE POINT FOR EACH MATCHING ANSWER. THEN FIND OUT YOUR SPOOKY SCORE BELOW.

1. Write the first color you think of ....

2. Name a film you love ....

3. Think of a girl's name beginning with "S" ....

4. Draw either a square, a circle, or a diamond ....

5. Name a song you like ....

6. Write a number between 1 and 10 ....

7. Name a famous person ....

8. Think of a month of the year ....

5-8: Wow! It's no mystery why you're BFFs!
You're on the same weirdly wonderful wavelength.

Date .... Time .... Place ....
This page was completed by ....

PICTURE PERFECT

CREATE A BEST FRIENDS GALLERY THAT YOU CAN LOOK
BACK ON TO REMEMBER ALL YOUR AMAZING PALS.

Get together with four friends and, in each picture frame over
the next five pages, draw a picture of each of them, starting
with yourself on page 19. You can create one picture each
or work together on your pals' portraits. Then, in the boxes
around the frame, write three positive words that describe
the person pictured. Don't forget to write the name of the
person you have drawn in the nameplate under each frame.

DRAW A PICTURE OF YOURSELF IN THE FRAME BELOW

....

....

....

Date .... Time .... Place ....
This page was completed by ....

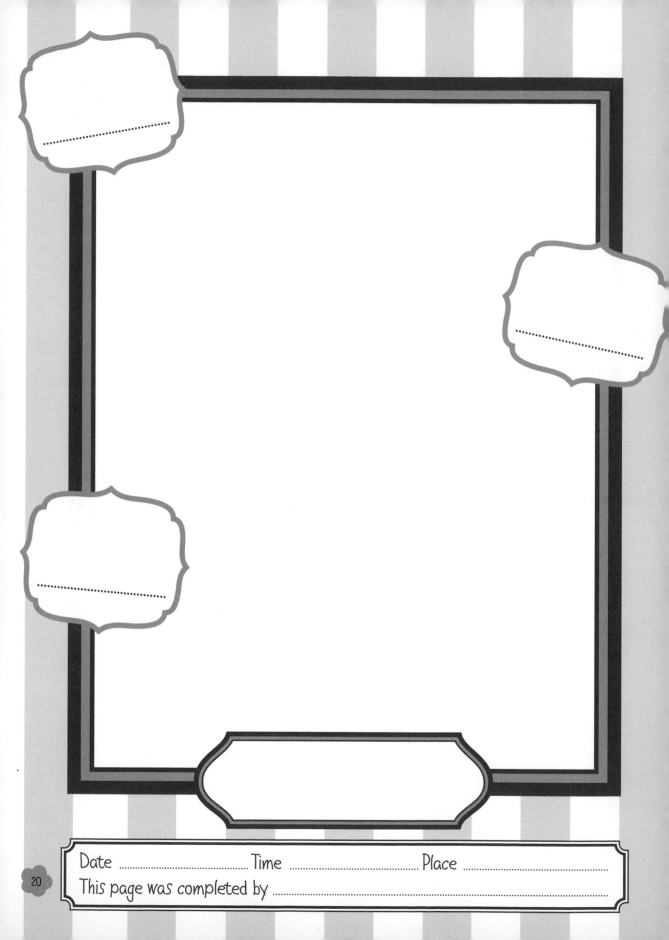

Date .... Time .... Place ....

This page was completed by ....

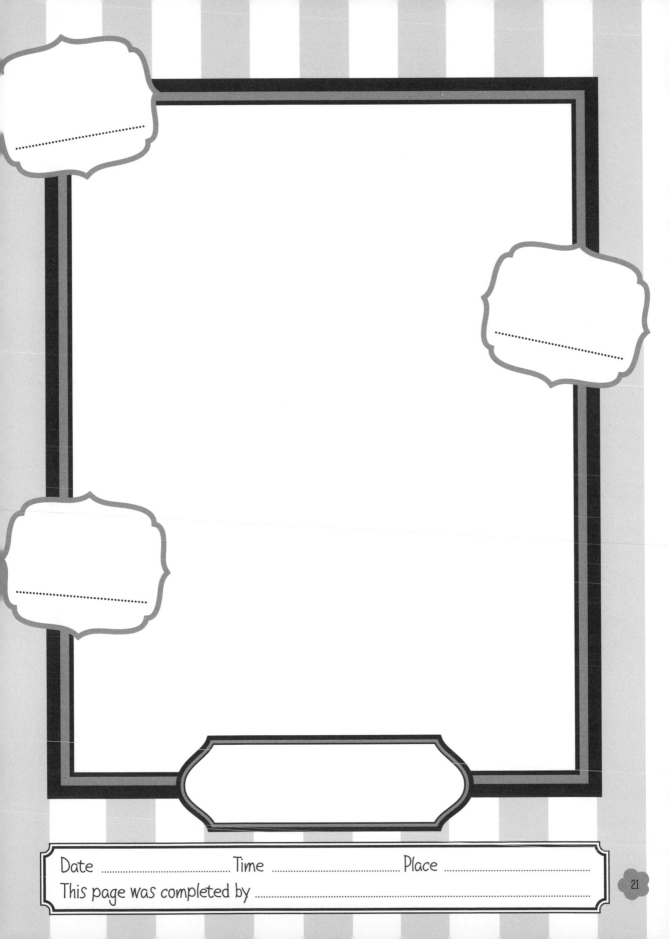

Date .... Time .... Place ....

This page was completed by ....

21

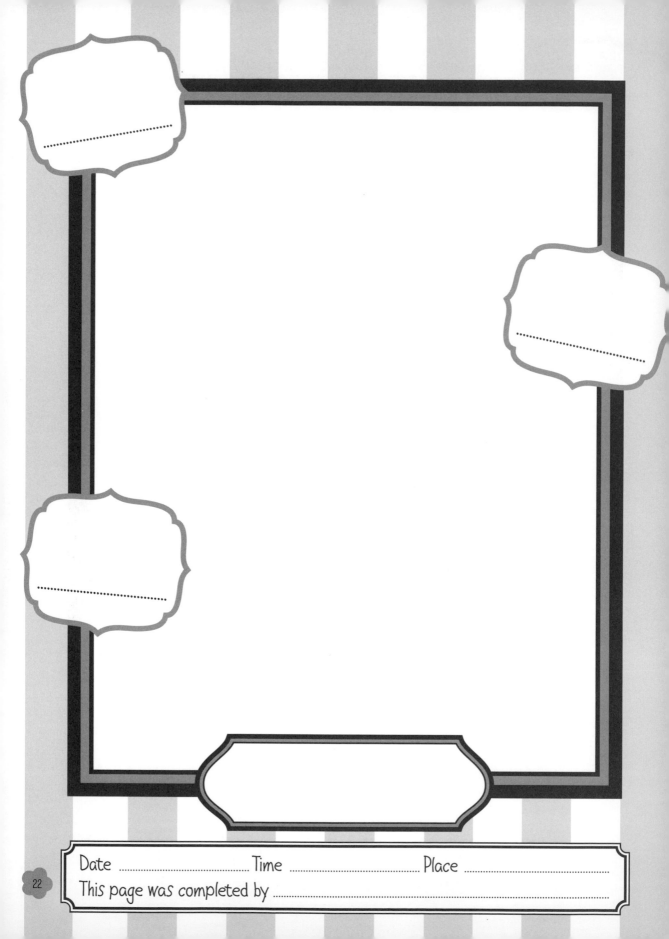

Date .... Time .... Place ....
This page was completed by ....

22

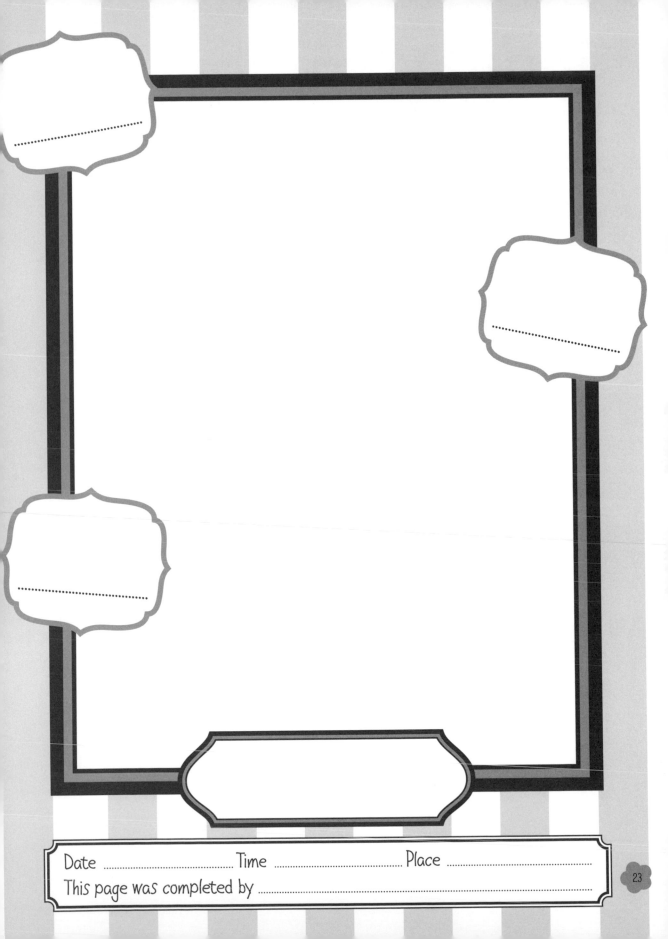

Date .... Time .... Place ....
This page was completed by ....

23

a Year OF THINGS TO DO TOGETHER

WHAT are YOUR PLANS FOR THE YEAR TO COME?

Write down 12 things that you and your BFF would like to do together. Make a funny video? Choreograph a killer dance routine? Bake a show-stopping cake? Check them off as you achieve them.

◇ January ....
....

◇ February ....
....

◇ March ....
....

◇ April ....
....

Date .... Time .... Place ....

◇ May ....
....

◇ June ....
....

◇ July ....
....

◇ August ....
....

◇ September ....
....

◇ October ....
....

◇ November ....
....

◇ December ....
....

These pages were completed by .... and ....

THINGS WE FIND SO ANNOYING

WHAT ANNOYS YOU MOST IN THE WHOLE WIDE WORLD?

Write down four things that really annoy you and your BFF in the first row, such as wasps or people kicking the back of your chair. Choose which thing from each pair is the most annoying, then decide which is the thing that annoys you both most of all in the world.

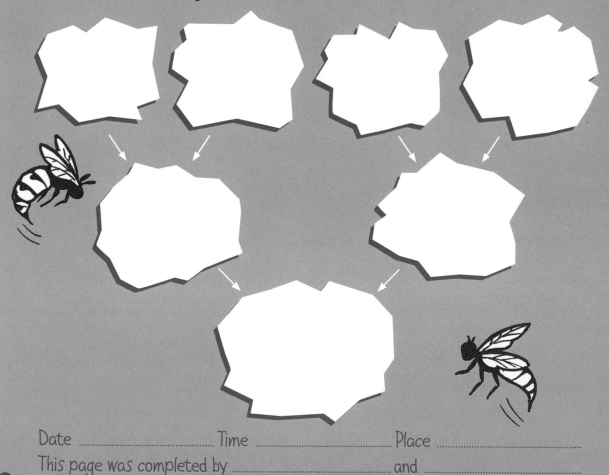

Date .... Time .... Place ....
This page was completed by .... and ....

a PROBLEM SHARED IS A PROBLEM HALVED

WE ALL HAVE THINGS WE SECRETLY WORRY ABOUT.
SHARING THOSE WORRIES IS A GREAT WAY
TO MAKE THEM LESS SCARY.

With a trusted friend, write your worries on the white
torn-paper panels on the next page. Ask your friend
to share her worries on the purple panels.

Just writing your worries down can make them less
scary. Sharing them with your BFF can make them so
tiny they hardly exist. When you've had a chance to chat
about what's been on your minds and have helped each
other see things differently, get rid of your worries once
and for all by carefully pulling out this page and tearing
it into tiny pieces.

TINY TIMES

WHAT IS THE VERY FIRST THING THAT YOU REMEMBER? FILL IN A MEMORY CLOUD AND SEE IF YOU CAN WORK OUT A ROUGH DATE FOR THE MEMORY. THEN, ASK YOUR BFF TO FILL IN HER OWN CLOUD.

Date ....

Time .... Place ....

My memory

...................'s memory

SLEEP FACT FILE

FILL IN THIS FACT FILE ABOUT YOUR SLEEPING HABITS.

Do you share your bedroom? Yes ◇ No ◇

If "yes," who do you share with? ....

Do you sleep with: One pillow? ◇ Two pillows? ◇ No pillows? ◇

Is there anything you can't sleep without? A cuddly toy? A glass of water? ....

What time do you normally go to bed? ....

What do you wear to bed? ....

What sleeping position do you find most comfortable?
On your front ◇ Curled up on your side ◇ On your back ◇

Have you ever:
Fallen out of bed? ◇
Sleepwalked? ◇
Woken yourself up snoring? ◇

Date .... Time .... Place ....
This page was completed by ....

NOW ASK YOUR BESTIE TO DO THE SAME BELOW.
WHEN YOU'VE FINISHED, TURN THE PAGE TO START
PLANNING YOUR BEST SLEEPOVER EVER!

Do you share your bedroom? Yes ◇ No ◇

If "yes," who do you share with? ....

Do you sleep with: One pillow? ◇ Two pillows? ◇ No pillows? ◇

Is there anything you can't sleep without? A cuddly toy? A glass of water? ....

What time do you normally go to bed? ....

What do you wear to bed? ....

What sleeping position do you find most comfortable?
On your front ◇ Curled up on your side ◇ On your back ◇

Have you ever:
Fallen out of bed? ◇
Sleepwalked? ◇
Woken yourself up snoring? ◇

Date .... Time .... Place ....
This page was completed by ....

SUPER SLEEPOVER PLANNER

FILL IN EACH CATEGORY BELOW TO PLAN YOUR BEST EVER SLEEPOVER TOGETHER.

WHEN WILL THE SLEEPOVER BE?

THEME (SUCH AS PAJAMA PARTY OR NAIL SPA):

MOVIE IDEAS:

WHAT TO WEAR (SUCH AS A COZY ROBE OR FLUFFY SLIPPERS):

Date .... Time .... Place ....

SNACKS (SUCH AS CUPCAKES OR SMOOTHIES):

GAMES:

ACTIVITIES (SUCH AS POLISHING NAILS OR BRAIDING HAIR):

RULES (SUCH AS NO WAKING EACH OTHER UP BEFORE 6 A.M.!):

WHO WILL BE THE FIRST ASLEEP?

WHO WILL BE THE FIRST AWAKE?

These pages were completed by .... and ....

FASHION STYLE CHALLENGE

YOUR BFF'S FAVE HAIRSTYLE

a. Short and chic
b. High ponytail
c. Boho braids
d. Loose and wavy

YOUR BFF'S TOP NAIL POLISH COLOR

a. Neon yellow
b. Simple and natural
c. Multicolored
d. Bright pink and glittery

YOUR BFF'S PERFECT PARTY OUTFIT

a. Rainbow crop top and yoga pants
b. Jeggings and a baggy T-shirt
c. Long, floaty skirt and a flowery top
d. Sequin dress and a matching clutch bag

This page was completed by ....

HOW WELL DO YOU AND YOUR BFF KNOW EACH OTHER'S STYLE?
CIRCLE THE OPTIONS THAT YOU THINK BEST DESCRIBE YOUR BFF'S
FASHION SENSE ON PAGES 34 AND 36. THEN GET YOUR BFF
TO DO THE SAME ABOUT YOU ON PAGES 35 AND 37.

WHEN YOU HAVE BOTH FILLED IN ALL YOUR QUESTIONS, CHECK OUT
PAGE 38 FOR YOUR TREND TYPES. WILL YOU AGREE WITH THEM?

Date .... Time .... Place ....

YOUR BFF'S FAVE HAIRSTYLE

a. Short and chic
b. High ponytail
c. Boho braids
d. Loose and wavy

YOUR BFF'S TOP NAIL POLISH COLOR

a. Neon yellow
b. Simple and natural
c. Multicolored
d. Bright pink and glittery

YOUR BFF'S PERFECT PARTY OUTFIT

a. Rainbow crop top and yoga pants
b. Jeggings and a baggy T-shirt
c. Long, floaty skirt and a flowery top
d. Sequin dress and a matching clutch bag

This page was completed by ....

YOUR BFF'S SHOPPING HOT SPOT

a. Main street
b. Discount store
c. Shopping mall
d. Designer boutique

YOUR BFF'S PREFERRED PATTERN

a. Leopard print
b. Geometric shapes
c. Pink and purple flowers
d. Sparkly swirls

YOUR BFF'S STAR SHOES

a. Platforms
b. Hi-tops
c. Flip-flops
d. Glittery pumps

YOUR BFF'S DREAM VACATION

a. An outdoor adventure
b. Drama summer camp
c. Art camp
d. Relaxing on a beach

This page was completed by ....

YOUR BFF'S SHOPPING HOT SPOT

a. Main street

b. Discount store

c. Shopping mall

d. Designer boutique

YOUR BFF'S PREFERRED PATTERN

a. Leopard print

b. Geometric shapes

c. Pink and purple flowers

d. Sparkly swirls

YOUR BFF'S STAR SHOES

a. Platforms

b. Hi-tops

c. Flip-flops

d. Glittery pumps

YOUR BFF'S DREAM VACATION

a. An outdoor adventure

b. Drama summer camp

c. Art camp

d. Relaxing on a beach

This page was completed by ....

FASHION STYLE CHALLENGE TREND TYPES

Mostly As: Bold babe

You love anything bright, bold, and interesting, from bright colors to action-packed adventures. You're not afraid to try new things, and you don't mind standing out from the crowd. But sometimes you're happy to take a back seat and be one of the gang, too.

Mostly Bs: Sporty star

You're always ready for action, whether out on the sports field or playing games with your friends. You don't have much time for fashion, and you prefer to feel comfy and free.

Mostly Cs: Happy hipster

You're fun-loving, creative, and dreamy. You love using your arty skills to add pretty touches to your look, such as a beaded necklace or a patterned headband. You sometimes have your head in the clouds, but your friends are usually there to bring you back down to earth.

Mostly Ds: Glam girl

One thing is for sure—you can't have enough glitter and sequins in your wardrobe! You love nothing more than dressing up with your friends and being pampered. You do have a serious side, though. You can sometimes be found writing all about your glamorous thoughts and dreams.

CHOICES, CHOICES

LOOK AT THE HEARTS BELOW AND COLOR IN YOUR FAVORITE OF EACH PAIR. GET YOUR BFF TO DO THE SAME THING IN THE COLUMN NEXT TO YOURS.

Date _____ Time _____ Place _____

Completed by _____

Completed by _____

I Wanna Be . . .

What does the future hold for you? Answer the questions on pages 40 and 42, and get your BFF to answer the same questions on pages 41 and 43.

It's your birthday. How do you celebrate?

a. By inviting my best friends to a multisports party
b. By starting on my new novel collection
c. By hosting a karaoke night with a big bunch of friends
d. By attending a bead-making workshop

What is your favorite subject at school?

a. PE
b. Math or Science
c. Drama or Music
d. Art

What would be your ideal weekend?

a. Swimming and gymnastics followed by trampolining
b. Getting to work on writing my latest book
c. Having some friends over to perform a musical I have written
d. Volunteering my help at the local animal shelter

This page was completed by ....

YOU WANNA BE . . .

THEN TURN TO PAGE 44 TO DISCOVER WHAT MIGHT LIE AHEAD FOR BOTH OF YOU AND IF YOUR DESTINIES ARE AS CLOSE AS YOU ARE. . . .

Date .... Time .... Place ....

IT'S YOUR BIRTHDAY. HOW DO YOU CELEBRATE?

a. By inviting my best friends to a multisports party
b. By starting on my new novel collection
c. By hosting a karaoke night with a big bunch of friends
d. By attending a bead-making workshop

WHAT IS YOUR FAVORITE SUBJECT AT SCHOOL?

a. PE
b. Math or Science
c. Drama or Music
d. Art

WHAT WOULD BE YOUR IDEAL WEEKEND?

a. Swimming and gymnastics followed by trampolining
b. Getting to work on writing my latest book
c. Having some friends over to perform a musical
   I have written
d. Volunteering my help at the local animal shelter

This page was completed by ....

WHICH OF THESE DRINKS WOULD YOU MOST LIKE TO HAVE?

a. A can of soda
b. A glass of purified water
c. A fruity mocktail
d. An organic smoothie

WHAT KIND OF FILMS DO YOU MOST LIKE TO WATCH?

a. Action thrillers
b. Documentaries
c. Talent shows
d. Comedies

HOW WOULD YOUR FRIENDS DESCRIBE YOU?

a. Adventurous
b. Clever
c. Fun and creative
d. Kind and caring

WHAT KIND OF SCHOOL STUDENT ARE YOU?

a. I spend most of the class fidgeting and daydreaming
b. I listen carefully and take detailed notes
c. I listen only when the teacher is talking about something interesting
d. I do pretty well, and I help my classmates out when they're stuck

WHICH OF THE FOLLOWING IS MOST IMPORTANT FOR THE FUTURE?

a. Having amazing stories to tell
b. An interesting and challenging career
c. Fame and fortune
d. Love and family

This page was completed by ....

WHICH OF THESE DRINKS WOULD YOU MOST LIKE TO HAVE?

a. A can of soda
b. A glass of purified water
c. A fruity mocktail
d. An organic smoothie

WHAT KIND OF FILMS DO YOU MOST LIKE TO WATCH?

a. Action thrillers
b. Documentaries
c. Talent shows
d. Comedies

HOW WOULD YOUR FRIENDS DESCRIBE YOU?

a. Adventurous
b. Clever
c. Fun and creative
d. Kind and caring

WHAT KIND OF SCHOOL STUDENT ARE YOU?

a. I spend most of the class fidgeting and daydreaming
b. I listen carefully and take detailed notes
c. I listen only when the teacher is talking about something interesting
d. I do pretty well, and I help my classmates out when they're stuck

WHICH OF THE FOLLOWING IS MOST IMPORTANT FOR THE FUTURE?

a. Having amazing stories to tell
b. An interesting and challenging career
c. Fame and fortune
d. Love and family

This page was completed by ....

we wanna be . . . results

Mostly As: All-action hero
You have a strong sense of adventure, so any career working in the great outdoors would be perfect, such as a nature conservationist, botanist (a plant specialist), or marine biologist. If you prefer working with people, you could also consider becoming a journalist, travel writer, or private detective.

Mostly Bs: Top dog
You enjoy studying, and you're not afraid of working hard. You are ambitious and would love a job that pays well but is also interesting and challenging. Your ideal job could be as a doctor, lawyer, architect, or scientist.

Mostly Cs: Superstar performer
You love to be center stage and to show off all your creative skills! With such a bold personality and passion for performing, there's a chance you could become famous one day, perhaps as an actor, musician, fashion designer, or film director.

Mostly Ds: Queen of hearts
You're a kind and generous person who likes to help others. A career working with people would suit you, for example as a nurse, teacher, or carer. If you are an animal-lover, a vet, zoologist, or animal control officer could be the ideal job for you.

AND THE WINNER IS . . .

IT'S TIME TO NOMINATE YOUR FAVORITE PEOPLE FOR A SET OF VERY SPECIAL PRIZES.

Do you have a friend who's always top of the class and is bound to become the next president? Or another friend who's great at singing and destined to be a chart-topping pop princess?

Turn the page and work together with your friend or a group of friends to draw a picture of the person you think should receive each award. Write the name underneath each portrait. You can nominate the same friend for different awards if you think she deserves it!

Date .... Time .... Place ....

WHO IS MOST LIKELY TO . . .

become president?

....

compose a chart-topping song?

....

work in fashion?

....

become a vet?

....

These pages were completed by ....

write a best-selling novel?

walk down the red carpet?

travel the world?

find a cure for a deadly disease?

WHO IS MOST LIKELY TO . . .

win a dance competition?

discover a new planet?

....

become an Olympic champion?

marry a prince?

....

These pages were completed by ....

become a famous artist?

....

become a celebrity chef?

....

wrestle an alligator?

....

climb Mount Everest?

....

FASHIONISTA or . . .

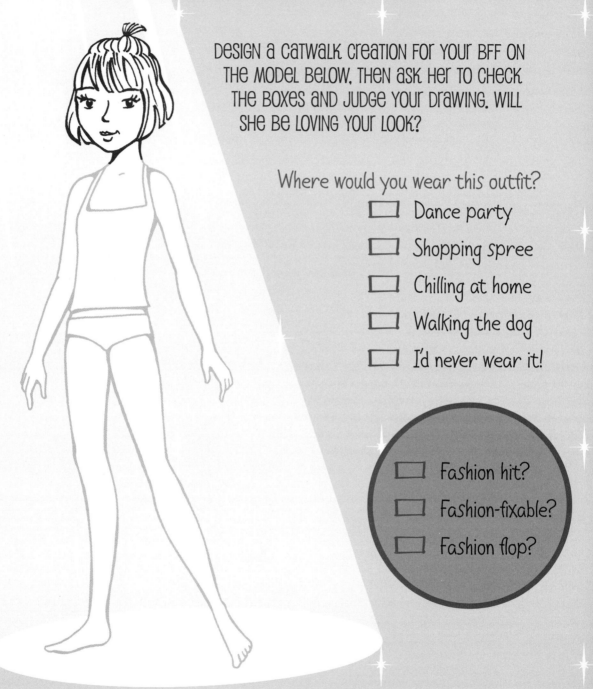

DESIGN a CATWALK CREATION FOR YOUR BFF ON THE MODEL BELOW, THEN ASK HER TO CHECK THE BOXES AND JUDGE YOUR DRAWING. WILL SHE BE LOVING YOUR LOOK?

Where would you wear this outfit?

- ☐ Dance party
- ☐ Shopping spree
- ☐ Chilling at home
- ☐ Walking the dog
- ☐ I'd never wear it!

- ☐ Fashion hit?
- ☐ Fashion-fixable?
- ☐ Fashion flop?

Date .... Time .... Place ....

This page was completed by ....

FASHION FLOP?

NOW IT'S YOUR TURN FOR THE DESIGNER TREATMENT. ASK YOUR BFF TO CREATE AN AMAZING ENSEMBLE FOR YOU ON THE MODEL. THEN CHECK THE BOXES AND GIVE HER YOUR DESIGNER DECISION.

Where would you wear this outfit?

- ☐ Dance party
- ☐ Shopping spree
- ☐ Chilling at home
- ☐ Walking the dog
- ☐ I'd never wear it!

- ☐ Fashion hit?
- ☐ Fashion-fixable?
- ☐ Fashion flop?

Date .... Time .... Place ....
This page was completed by ....

HAPPY VACATIONS

Where was the best place you ever went on vacation?

....

....

How did you get there?
Car ◇ Bus ◇ Plane ◇ Boat ◇ Train ◇

Where did you stay?
Apartment or house ◇ Tent ◇ Camper ◇ Hotel ◇

What did you do there?

....

....

....

Who did you go with?

....

Date .... Time .... Place ....
This page was completed by ....

GRAB YOUR BFF AND FILL IN THESE PAGES WITH DETAILS OF YOUR HAPPIEST-EVER VACATION. CHOOSE A PAGE EACH TO COMPLETE.

Where was the best place you ever went on vacation?

....

....

How did you get there?
Car ◇ Bus ◇ Plane ◇ Boat ◇ Train ◇

Where did you stay?
Apartment or house ◇ Tent ◇ Camper ◇ Hotel ◇

What did you do there?

....

....

....

Who did you go with?

....

Date .... Time .... Place ....
This page was completed by ....

TRIP OF A LIFETIME

IMAGINE YOU AND YOUR BEST FRIEND ARE GOING ON VACATION TOGETHER. FILL IN THE BOXES BELOW TO PLAN YOUR DREAM TRIP. YOU CAN GO WHEREVER YOU LIKE AND DO WHATEVER YOU WANT!

WHERE WOULD YOU LIKE TO GO?

HOW WOULD YOU GET THERE?

WHERE WOULD YOU STAY?

WOULD YOU SHARE A ROOM OR HAVE YOUR OWN ROOM?

Date .... Time .... Place ....

WHO WOULD GO WITH YOU?

HOW WOULD YOU SPEND
EACH DAY?

WHAT KIND OF PLACES WOULD
YOU LIKE TO VISIT?

WHAT WOULD YOU EAT?

WHAT WOULD YOU WEAR?

WHAT SOUVENIRS WOULD YOU BUY?

These pages were completed by .... and ....

Face Your Fears

Spiders ◇ Slugs ◇ Wasps ◇ Worms ◇ Caterpillars ◇

Snakes ◇ Rats ◇ Dogs ◇ Bats ◇ Wolves ◇

Speaking in public ◇ Singing on stage ◇ School tests ◇

Dark places ◇ Noisy places ◇ Crowded places ◇ High places ◇

Ghosts ◇ Zombies ◇ Vampires ◇ Ogres ◇ Trolls ◇

Airplanes ◇ Boats ◇ Fast cars ◇ Roller coasters ◇

Thunder ◇ Injections ◇ Being sick ◇ Being stuck in an elevator ◇

Walking into a room full of people I don't know ◇

Walking into a room full of people I do know ◇

Realizing my skirt is tucked into my underwear ◇

Tripping in front of a crowd of people ◇

Date .... Time .... Place ....
This page was completed by ....

WHAT are YOU MOST afraID OF, anD WHaT SETS YOUR BFF'S HEART THUMPING WITH FEAR? CHECK THE BOXES ON PAGE 56 AND aSK YOUR BFF TO DO THE SAME BELOW. THEN UNDERLINE YOUR GREATEST FEAR OF ALL TIME.

Spiders ◇ Slugs ◇ Wasps ◇ Worms ◇ Caterpillars ◇

Snakes ◇ Rats ◇ Dogs ◇ Bats ◇ Wolves ◇

Speaking in public ◇ Singing on stage ◇ School tests ◇

Dark places ◇ Noisy places ◇ Crowded places ◇ High places ◇

Ghosts ◇ Zombies ◇ Vampires ◇ Ogres ◇ Trolls ◇

Airplanes ◇ Boats ◇ Fast cars ◇ Roller coasters ◇

Thunder ◇ Injections ◇ Being sick ◇ Being stuck in an elevator ◇

Walking into a room full of people I don't know ◇

Walking into a room full of people I do know ◇

Realizing my skirt is tucked into my underwear ◇

Tripping over in front of a crowd of people ◇

Date .... Time .... Place ....
This page was completed by ....

FABULOUS FEASTS

STARTER
TOMATO SOUP
GARLIC BREAD
CARROT STICKS AND DIP

MAIN COURSE
SPAGHETTI BOLOGNESE
CHEESEBURGER
VEGETABLE CURRY
SUSHI SELECTION
CHEESE PIZZA

SIDE DISHES
PEAS
FRIES
GREEN SALAD
BROCCOLI
FRUIT SALAD

DESSERT
CHOCOLATE BROWNIE
ICE CREAM SUNDAE
COOKIE

DRINKS
LEMONADE
SODA
WATER
MILKSHAKE

BIRTHDAY CAKE
CHOCOLATE FUDGE
RAINBOW PIÑATA
CUPCAKE CREATIONS

Ask your BFF to rate your choices. Feast fit for a queen? YUM! ◇ Dog's dinner? YUCK! ◇

Date .... Time .... Place ....

This page was completed by ....

IF YOU WERE PLANNING A SPECIAL BIRTHDAY MEAL FOR YOUR BFF, WHAT WOULD SHE MOST LIKE TO EAT AND DRINK? CIRCLE YOUR CHOICES FOR HER ON PAGE 58, AND ASK HER TO DO THE SAME FOR YOU BELOW.

STARTER
TOMATO SOUP
GARLIC BREAD
CARROT STICKS AND DIP

MAIN COURSE
SPAGHETTI BOLOGNESE
CHEESEBURGER
VEGETABLE CURRY
SUSHI SELECTION
CHEESE PIZZA

SIDE DISHES
PEAS
FRIES
GREEN SALAD
BROCCOLI
FRUIT SALAD

DESSERT
CHOCOLATE BROWNIE
ICE CREAM SUNDAE
COOKIE

DRINKS
LEMONADE
SODA
WATER
MILKSHAKE

BIRTHDAY CAKE
CHOCOLATE FUDGE
RAINBOW PIÑATA
CUPCAKE CREATIONS

Ask your BFF to rate your choices. Feast fit for a queen? YUM! ◇ Dog's dinner? YUCK! ◇

Date .... Time .... Place ....

This page was completed by ....

GO ON, I DARE YOU!

Would you ever . . .	NEVER! 0 points	MAYBE 1 point	DEFINITELY! 2 points
touch a snake?	◇	◇	◇
jump off a high diving board?	◇	◇	◇
spend the night in a cave?	◇	◇	◇
take a ride in a jet fighter plane?	◇	◇	◇
go rock climbing?	◇	◇	◇
swim outside when it's snowing?	◇	◇	◇
eat snails?	◇	◇	◇
sing a song on live TV?	◇	◇	◇

Score

....

These pages were completed by .... and ....

WHO IS THE MOST DARING—YOU OR YOUR BFF? CHECK THE BOXES ON PAGE 60 AND ASK HER TO DO THE SAME BELOW, AND ADD UP YOUR SCORES AT THE END.

Date .... Time .... Place ....

Would you ever . . .	NEVER! 0 points	MAYBE 1 point	DEFINITELY! 2 points
touch a snake?	◇	◇	◇
jump off a high diving board?	◇	◇	◇
spend the night in a cave?	◇	◇	◇
take a ride in a jet fighter plane?	◇	◇	◇
go rock climbing?	◇	◇	◇
swim outside when it's snowing?	◇	◇	◇
eat snails?	◇	◇	◇
sing a song on live TV?	◇	◇	◇

Score

....

WARNING!
The daredevil of our duo is:

....

BEST FRIEND STAR awards

ONE THING'S FOR SURE, YOUR BFF IS A STAR! WRITE DOWN THE FIVE THINGS YOU LIKE BEST ABOUT HER IN THE STARS BELOW.

Date .... Time .... Place ....
This page was completed by ....

WHAT DOES YOUR BFF LIKE BEST ABOUT YOU? ASK HER TO FILL IN THE STARS BELOW.

Hide your answers from each other, and hold your own mini awards ceremony. Drumrolls are essential!

Date .... Time .... Place ....
This page was completed by ....

63

I CaN . . .

DO YOU HAVE ANY HIDDEN TALENTS?
CHECK OFF EACH THING BELOW THAT YOU CAN DO.

	easy peasy!	no can do!
Make a sound by rolling your "r"s	◇	◇
Rub your tummy and pat your head at the same time	◇	◇
Do the splits	◇	◇
Raise one eyebrow	◇	◇
Flare your nostrils	◇	◇
Do a backbend	◇	◇
Touch your toes without bending your legs	◇	◇
Wiggle your ears	◇	◇

I'M GOING TO PRACTICE ....

Date .... Time .... Place ....
This page was completed by ....

CaN YOU?

ask YOUR BFF TO CHECK OFF WHAT SHE CaN DO BELOW. IF SHE HAS SKILLS YOU DON'T SHARE, ask HER TO TEACH YOU. WHAT COULD YOU TEACH HER TO DO?

	EaSY PEaSY!	NO CaN DO!
Make a sound by rolling your "r"s	◇	◇
Rub your tummy and pat your head at the same time	◇	◇
Do the splits	◇	◇
Raise one eyebrow	◇	◇
Flare your nostrils	◇	◇
Do a backbend	◇	◇
Touch your toes without bending your legs	◇	◇
Wiggle your ears	◇	◇

I'M GOING TO Practice ....

Date .... Time .... Place ....

This page was completed by ....

65

Purr-Fect Pals

FILL IN THE PET FACT FILE BELOW, EITHER ABOUT YOUR
FAVORITE PET OR ONE THAT YOU DREAM OF OWNING.

Pet's name ....

Pet's age ....

Type of animal ....

Boy ◇   Girl ◇   Not sure! ◇

Color of fur ....

Color of eyes ....

Favorite food ....

Cutest trick ....

Naughtiest moment ....

....

....

Date .... Time .... Place ....

This page was completed by ....

GET YOUR BFF TO FILL IN THIS PAGE, AND WHEN YOU'RE DONE,
DRAW A PICTURE OF YOUR PET IN EACH PHOTO FRAME.

Pet's name ....

Pet's age ....

Type of animal ....

Boy ◇   Girl ◇   Not sure! ◇

Color of fur ....

Color of eyes ....

Favorite food ....

Cutest trick ....

Naughtiest moment ....

....

....

Date .... Time .... Place ....

This page was completed by ....

HAND IN HAND

Decorate your hand drawings with henna patterns and color the nails in each other's favorite shade.

Date .... Time .... Place ....
This page was completed by ....

CREATE A LASTING MEMORY OF YOUR FRIENDSHIP BY TRACING AROUND YOUR BFF'S HAND IN THE SPACE BELOW, AND LET HER TRACE AROUND YOUR HAND IN THE OPPOSITE SPACE.

Why not add a friendship bracelet to your drawings or design a beautiful friendship ring?

Date .... Time .... Place ....

This page was completed by ....

OUR DREAM PARTY

IMAGINE YOU AND YOUR BFF ARE ALLOWED TO PLAN YOUR PERFECT PARTY. NO RULES, NO BUDGET, NO GROWN-UPS!

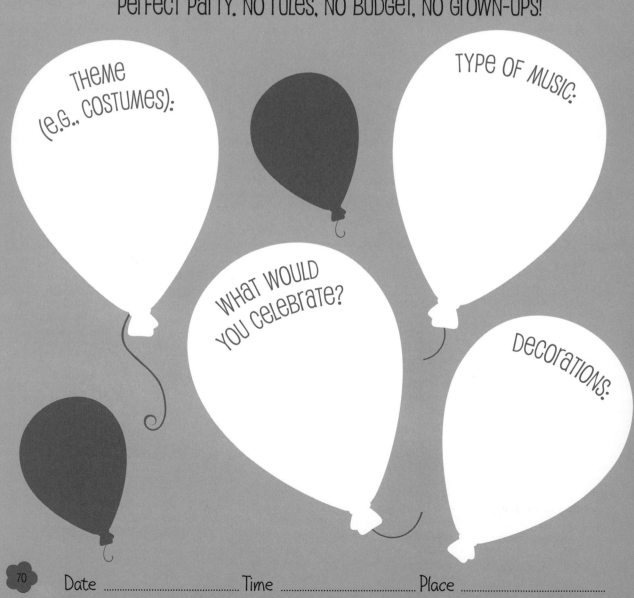

THEME (E.G., COSTUMES):

TYPE OF MUSIC:

WHAT WOULD YOU CELEBRATE?

DECORATIONS:

Date .... Time .... Place ....

ENTERTAINMENT (E.G., FAVE BAND):

FOOD:

DRINKS:

WHO IS YOUR BFF'S DREAM GUEST?

WHAT WILL YOU WEAR?

WHO IS YOUR DREAM GUEST?

These pages were completed by .... and ....

I ♥ TV...

FILL IN YOUR TOP FIVE TV SHOWS BELOW, AND ASK YOUR BFF TO DO THE SAME ON THE NEXT PAGE.

1.

2.

3.

4.

5.

Date .... Time .... Place ....
This page was completed by ....

YOU ♥ TV

COMPARE YOUR ANSWERS WHEN YOU'VE FINISHED AND CIRCLE ANY THAT ARE THE SAME.

1.

2.

3.

4.

5.

Date .... Time .... Place ....

This page was completed by ....

73

SIGNATURE STYLE

WHAT DOES YOUR HANDWRITING SAY ABOUT YOUR PERSONALITY? WRITE IN THE BOXES BELOW AND ASK YOUR FRIEND TO DO THE SAME ON THE OPPOSITE PAGE. THEN TURN TO PAGE 76 TO START ANALYZING EACH OTHER'S HANDWRITING.

First, write your name in the box below:

Next, copy the words "Best Friends Forever" below:

Date .... Time .... Place ....

This page was completed by ....

First, write your name in the box below:

Next, copy the words "Best Friends Forever" below:

WHAT DO YOU THINK? IS YOUR HANDWRITING VERY DIFFERENT FROM YOUR BFF'S, OR IS IT HARD TO TELL YOUR WRITING APART?

TURN OVER TO FIND OUT WHAT YOUR WIGGLES AND SQUIGGLES MIGHT MEAN.

Date .... Time .... Place ....

This page was completed by ....

SIGNATURE STYLE ANSWERS

WHAT SIZE IS THE HANDWRITING?

Large letters

This writer has a big personality and enjoys being the center of attention.

Small letters

This handwriting can show shyness and that the writer might be good at concentrating.

DO THE LETTERS SLOPE OR STAND UPRIGHT?

Slope to the left

This writer likes to spend time on her own.

Slope to the right

Writing that slopes to the right shows an open and sociable person.

Stand upright

The writer is practical and independent.

LOOK OUT FOR THESE CHARACTERISTICS IN EACH OTHER'S WRITING STYLE AND READ ABOUT WHAT THEY MEAN.

WHAT SHAPE ARE THE LETTERS?

Cursive letters — These show a logical person who makes decisions very carefully.

Loopy or rounded letters — This handwriting reveals an artistic and imaginative mind.

Pointed letters — Writing like this comes from a clever, curious, and quick-thinking person.

IS THE WRITING STYLE MESSY OR NEAT?

Neat — A reliable, confident, and friendly person wrote this!

Messy — Writing like this shows a private person who likes to keep to herself.

NAME GAME

Write down your top ten girls' names and top ten boys' names below. Ask your bestie to make her own list on page 79.

GIRLS' NAMES

1. ....
2. ....
3. ....
4. ....
5. ....
6. ....
7. ....
8. ....
9. ....
10. ....

BOYS' NAMES

1. ....
2. ....
3. ....
4. ....
5. ....
6. ....
7. ....
8. ....
9. ....
10. ....

Date .... Time .... Place ....

This page was completed by ....

GIRLS' NAMES	BOYS' NAMES
1.	1. ....
2.	2. ....
3.	3. ....
4.	4. ....
5.	5. ....
6.	6. ....
7.	7. ....
8.	8. ....
9.	9. ....
10.	10. ....

UNDERLINE ANY NAMES THAT YOU BOTH LIKE, THEN DECIDE YOUR JOINT FAVORITE NAMES AND WRITE THEM BELOW:

FAVE GIRLS' NAME	FAVE BOYS' NAME
....	....

Date .... Time .... Place ....

This page was completed by ....

TOP 10 TUNES

MAKE A PLAYLIST OF WHAT YOU THINK ARE YOUR BFF'S ALL-TIME FAVORITE SONGS OR PIECES OF MUSIC, THEN ASK HER TO MAKE A LIST OF YOUR FAVES ON THE NEXT PAGE.

	HIT	MISS
1.	◇	◇
2.	◇	◇
3.	◇	◇
4.	◇	◇
5.	◇	◇
6.	◇	◇
7.	◇	◇
8.	◇	◇
9.	◇	◇
10.	◇	◇

THEN LET HER DECIDE IF EACH SONG YOU HAVE CHOSEN IS A HIT OR A MISS BY CHECKING ONE OF THE BOXES, AND YOU CAN DO THE SAME FOR HER LIST ON THE NEXT PAGE.

Date .... Time .... Place ....

This page was completed by ....

	HIT	MISS
1.	◇	◇
2.	◇	◇
3.	◇	◇
4.	◇	◇
5.	◇	◇
6.	◇	◇
7.	◇	◇
8.	◇	◇
9.	◇	◇
10.	◇	◇

CAN YOU AGREE ON YOUR JOINT
TOP TWO TUNES OF ALL TIME?
....

Date .... Time .... Place ....
This page was completed by ....

 # SO EMOJI-ONAL!

My little sister is so annoying, but when I tell her to stop, I get in trouble.

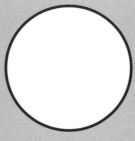

I went to school without realizing I had toothpaste all down my top.

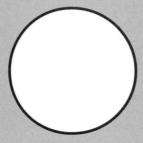

I got a perfect score on my math test.

I left my favorite hoodie on the bus and it's lost forever.

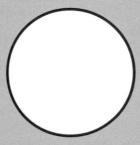

I waved at my BFF only to realize it wasn't her at all!

I wrote a secret text message to my BF and accidentally sent it to my grandma.

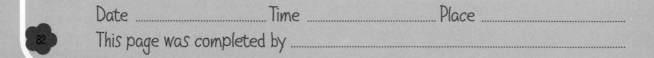

Date .... Time .... Place ....

This page was completed by ....

everyone LOVeS an emOJI! THeY are a FUN WaY TO express your emOTIONS. read eacH SITUaTION ON Page 82. THeN Draw an emOJI TO maTcH HOW IT MIGHT maKe YOU FeeL. ask your BFF TO DO THe same BeLOW.

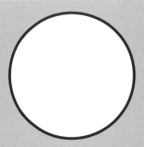

My little sister is so annoying, but when I tell her to stop, I get in trouble.

I went to school without realizing I had toothpaste all down my top.

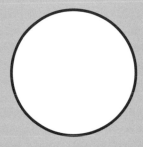

I got a perfect score on my math test.

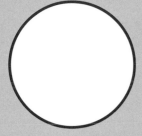

I left my favorite hoodie on the bus and it's lost forever.

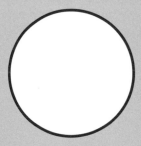

I waved at my BFF only to realize it wasn't her at all!

I wrote a secret text message to my BFF and accidentally sent it to my grandma.

Date .... Time .... Place ....
This page was completed by ....

83

MOVIE MATCH

WHAT WOULD BE YOUR TOP FIVE CHOICES FOR A MOVIE NIGHT WITH YOUR BFF? WRITE THEM BELOW, AND ASK HER TO FILL IN HER CHOICES ON THE OPPOSITE PAGE.

1.

2.

3.

4.

5.

Date .... Time .... Place ....

This page was completed by ....

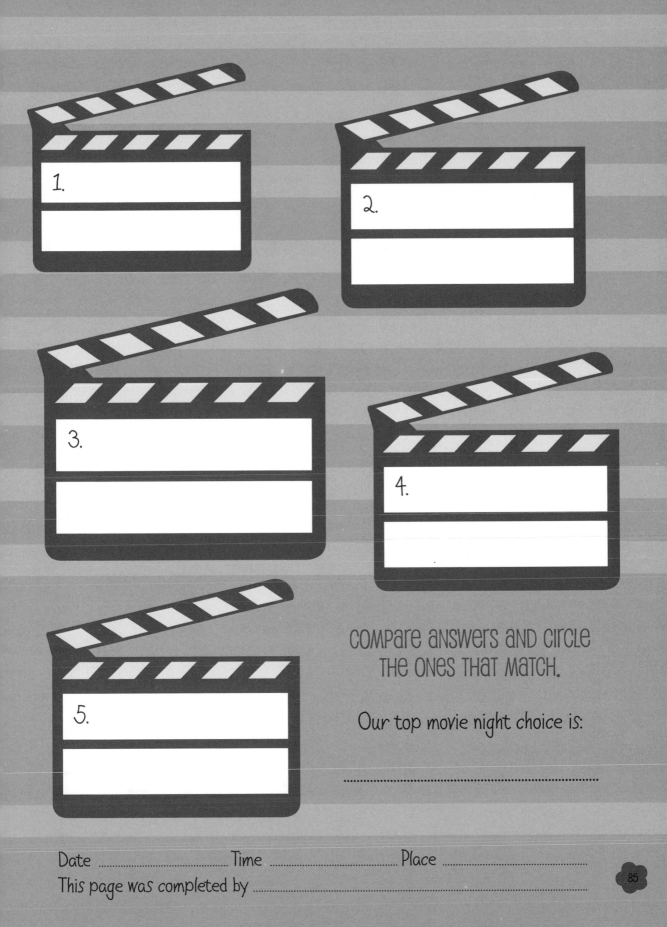

1.

2.

3.

4.

5.

COMPARE ANSWERS AND CIRCLE
THE ONES THAT MATCH.

Our top movie night choice is:

....

Date .... Time .... Place ....

This page was completed by ....

WHICH ANIMAL ARE YOU?

WHAT WOULD BE YOUR BFF'S IDEAL JOB?

a. An actor
b. An inventor
c. A businesswoman
d. An artist

WHERE WOULD SHE MOST LIKE TO LIVE?

a. She'd like to travel around
b. In a forest
c. In a big city
d. In the countryside

WHICH OF THESE ACTIVITIES WOULD SHE PREFER?

a. Hanging out with friends
b. Reading a book
c. Playing sports
d. Painting a picture

 This page was completed by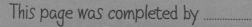

IF YOUR BFF WAS AN ANIMAL, WHAT WOULD SHE BE? ANSWER THE QUESTIONS ABOUT YOUR BFF ON PAGES 86 AND 88, AND GET YOUR BFF TO DO THE SAME ON PAGES 87 AND 89. THEN TURN TO PAGE 90 TO DISCOVER YOUR TRUE INNER ANIMALS.

Date .... Time .... Place ....

WHAT WOULD BE YOUR BFF'S IDEAL JOB?

a. An actor
b. An inventor
c. A businesswoman
d. An artist

WHERE WOULD SHE MOST LIKE TO LIVE?

a. She'd like to travel around
b. In a forest
c. In a big city
d. In the countryside

WHICH OF THESE ACTIVITIES WOULD SHE PREFER?

a. Hanging out with friends
b. Reading a book
c. Playing sports
d. Painting a picture

This page was completed by 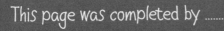 ....

WHICH OF THESE DESSERTS WOULD YOU ORDER FOR YOUR BFF?

a. Apple pie

b. Fruit salad

c. Chocolate fudge ice cream sundae

d. Vanilla cupcakes

WHICH OF THESE COLORS DOES SHE LIKE THE MOST?

a. Yellow

b. Blue

c. Red

d. Purple

SHE MOST ENJOYS READING . . .

a. Comics

b. Novels

c. Newspapers

d. Magazines

WHICH WORDS WOULD YOU CHOOSE TO DESCRIBE YOUR BFF?

a. Silly and fun

b. Interesting and clever

c. Bold and brave

d. Kind and creative

This page was completed by ....

WHICH OF THESE DESSERTS WOULD YOU ORDER FOR YOUR BFF?

a. Apple pie
b. Fruit salad
c. Chocolate fudge ice cream sundae
d. Vanilla cupcakes

WHICH OF THESE COLORS DOES SHE LIKE THE MOST?

a. Yellow
b. Blue
c. Red
d. Purple

SHE MOST ENJOYS READING . . .

a. Comics
b. Novels
c. Newspapers
d. Magazines

WHICH WORDS WOULD YOU CHOOSE TO DESCRIBE YOUR BFF?

a. Silly and fun
b. Interesting and clever
c. Bold and brave
d. Kind and creative

This page was completed by ....

Mostly As: OOH AAH! You're a chimpanzee. There's no doubt about it—monkeying around is your top priority! You are bursting with energy and always have lots of exciting plans and ideas.

Mostly Bs: HOOT HOOT! You're an owl. Clever and wise, you can usually be found with your head buried in a book or wowing your friends with interesting stories and fascinating facts.

Mostly Cs: ROAAR! You're a lion. As leader of the pack you love to be in charge, and you're not afraid to say what you really think. You stick up for your friends, and you're always there for them.

Mostly Ds: MEOW! You're a kitten. You're kind, gentle, and thoughtful, with an arty, creative streak, too. You're just as happy on your own as you are with a group of close friends.

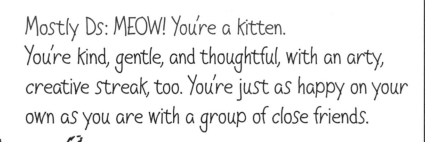

THaT was SO EMBaRRaSSING!

RECORD THE FIVE MOST EMBARRASSING MOMENTS YOU'VE HAD TOGETHER. BELIEVE IT OR NOT, YOU'LL FORGET THEM ONE DAY!

Date .... Time .... Place ....

1.

2.

3.

4.

5.

This page was completed by .... and ....

OODLES OF DOODLES

DOODLE THE FIRST THING THAT COMES INTO YOUR HEAD:

This page was completed by ....

THE WAY YOU DRAW AND DOODLE CAN SAY A LOT ABOUT YOUR PERSONALITY. HAVE FUN DOODLING IN THE BOXES ON PAGES 92 AND 94. ASK YOUR FRIEND TO DO THE SAME ON PAGES 93 AND 95. THEN TURN TO PAGE 96 TO SEE WHAT YOU'VE REVEALED!

Date .... Time .... Place ....

DOODLE THE FIRST THING THAT COMES INTO YOUR HEAD:

This page was completed by ....

NOW DOODLE A STAR, OR MORE THAN ONE STAR:

DRAW A HOUSE, OR MORE THAN ONE HOUSE, BELOW:

This page was completed by ....

NOW DOODLE A STAR, OR MORE THAN ONE STAR:

DRAW A HOUSE, OR MORE THAN ONE HOUSE, BELOW:

This page was completed by ....

OODLES OF DOODLES: RESULTS

Now take a look at each other's doodles. Check the boxes below that apply to your drawings to reveal your true personalities.

Draw a Doodle	ME	BFF
Flowers and hearts You are a kind, sensitive girl who loves a hug.	◇	◇
Animals An animal-lover, you are caring and thoughtful.	◇	◇
Faces You have a good sense of humor and like to be the center of attention.	◇	◇
Geometric shapes You are a problem solver and enjoy being in control.	◇	◇
Wiggly lines or swirls Often lost in your own thoughts, you are arty and creative.	◇	◇
Zigzags You are full of energy and like to get things done.	◇	◇

Rising Stars

	Me	BFF

There are lots of little stars.
This means you are a happy and optimistic person. ◇ ◇

There is one big star.
You are ambitious and strong-minded. ◇ ◇

Your star is neat and symmetrical.
You are clear-minded and good at being organized. ◇ ◇

Your star is drawn with sketchy lines.
This means you are creative and energetic. ◇ ◇

Home Sweet Home

	Me	BFF

Your house is standing alone.
You are happy to be in your own company. ◇ ◇

You have drawn more than one house.
You are sociable and outgoing. ◇ ◇

Your house's windows have no curtains or shutters.
You are open and honest. ◇ ◇

The windows have curtains or shutters.
You sometimes try to hide your feelings. ◇ ◇

DECISIONS . . . DECISIONS

DECIDE WHICH OF THESE TRICKY CHOICES YOU AND YOUR BFF WOULD RATHER DO IF YOU HAD TO. . . .

	ME	BFF
or Be invisible	◇	◇
Be able to fly	◇	◇
or Wear a heavy coat in a heatwave	◇	◇
Wear a swimsuit in the snow	◇	◇
or Eat a dead cockroach	◇	◇
Eat a live worm	◇	◇
or Jump into a pool of strawberry Jell-O	◇	◇
Lie in a warm bath of melted chocolate	◇	◇
or Not speak to your BFF for a whole year	◇	◇
Trip in front of your crush	◇	◇
or Camp out in the freezing Arctic	◇	◇
Camp out in the tropical jungle	◇	◇
or Never watch TV again	◇	◇
Never listen to music again	◇	◇

Date .... Time .... Place ....
This page was completed by .... and ....

secret codes

WRITE SECRET MESSAGES TO YOUR BFF USING
THE REVERSE ALPHABET CODE—IT'S SUPER EASY!

READ THE INSTRUCTIONS BELOW,
THEN TURN TO PAGE 100 TO HAVE A GO.

1. Start by writing out all the letters in the alphabet. Then, underneath,
write all the letters of the alphabet in the reverse order, like this:

A B C D E F G H I J K L M N O P Q R S T U V W X Y Z
Z Y X W V U T S R Q P O N M L K J I H G F E D C B A

Write the alphabet in the
reverse order, starting here.

2. To write your message, every time you use the letter A, you replace
it with the letter Z, or when you use B, you replace it with Y, and so on.
Here is an example:

H V X I V G   N V H H Z T V
S E C R E T   M E S S A G E

NOW IT'S TIME TO PRACTICE YOUR CODE WRITING! WORK OUT THE
REVERSE ALPHABET CODE WORD FOR EACH PICTURE BELOW, THEN
WRITE A SECRET MESSAGE TO YOUR BFF AND LET HER DECODE IT.

SECRET MESSAGE

DECODED MESSAGE

Date .... Time .... Place ....

The codes for these items are: HORKKVIH, YFEGVIUORVH, and HGZIH.

ASK YOUR BFF TO DO THE SAME ON THIS PAGE.

SECRET MESSAGE

DECODED MESSAGE

These pages were completed by .... and ....

The codes for these are: YLEGOV, SVZIGH, and UOLDVIH.

FRIENDSHIP FORTUNE WHEEL

LIVING IN . . . .

WORKING OR STUDYING?

LIVING WITH . . . .

PROUDEST ACHIEVEMENT . . . .

BEST FRIENDS WITH . . . .

STILL CAN'T . . . .

WILL HAVE MET . . . .

LOVES TO . . . .

Date .... Time .... Place ....

This page was completed by ....

WHAT WILL YOUR BFF BE DOING IN TEN YEARS' TIME? WRITE HER NAME IN THE CENTER OF THE WHEEL OF FORTUNE ON PAGE 102 AND YOUR PREDICTIONS IN EACH SECTION. ASK YOUR BFF TO DO THE SAME FOR YOU ON THIS PAGE.

WORKING OR STUDYING?

LIVING IN . . . .

LIVING WITH . . . .

PROUDEST ACHIEVEMENT . . . .

BEST FRIENDS WITH . . . .

STILL CAN'T . . . .

WILL HAVE MET . . . .

LOVES TO . . . .

Date .... Time .... Place ....

This page was completed by ....

BIRTHDAY WISH LIST

	OOH, YES PLEASE!	ERR, NO THANKS!
A nail-art kit	◇	◇
A funky shoulder bag	◇	◇
A new phone case	◇	◇
A book by her favorite author	◇	◇
A computer game	◇	◇
A new pair of headphones	◇	◇
A craft kit	◇	◇
A glittery T-shirt	◇	◇
A lockable diary	◇	◇
A friendship bracelet	◇	◇

Score
10

Date .... Time .... Place ....

This page was completed by ....

104

DO YOU KNOW WHAT'S ON YOUR BFF'S BIRTHDAY LIST?
CHECK WHETHER YOU THINK YOUR BFF WOULD LOVE OR HATE
THE GIFTS ON PAGE 104 AND ASK HER TO DO THE SAME FOR YOU
BELOW. NOW SWAP LISTS, COUNT UP ALL THE CORRECT ANSWERS,
AND RECORD YOUR SCORES. WHO SCORED THE HIGHEST?

	OOH, YES PLEASE!	ERR, NO THANKS!
A nail-art kit	◇	◇
A funky shoulder bag	◇	◇
A new phone case	◇	◇
A book by her favorite author	◇	◇
A computer game	◇	◇
A new pair of headphones	◇	◇
A craft kit	◇	◇
A glittery T-shirt	◇	◇
A lockable diary	◇	◇
A friendship bracelet	◇	◇

Score

10

Date .... Time .... Place ....

This page was completed by ....

SILLY SKETCHES

Draw your friend . . .

with your eyes shut.

with two pens.

with the hand you don't usually use.

with the page upside down.

Date .... Time .... Place ....

This page was completed by ....

DRAW FOUR PORTRAITS OF YOUR FRIEND ON PAGE 106, WHILE SHE MAKES SIMILAR CRAZY DOODLES OF YOU ON THIS PAGE!

DRAW YOUR FRIEND . . .

with your eyes shut.

with two pens.

with the hand you don't usually use.

with the page upside down.

Date .... Time .... Place ....

This page was completed by ....

MEMORY TEST

WHAT KIND OF MEMORY DO YOU HAVE? DO YOU REMEMBER WORDS OR PICTURES MORE EASILY?

Look at this page for one minute, while your friend looks at page 109. Then shut the book and write down everything you can remember.

RABBIT	HOUSE	BRACELET	TREE	BAG
BED	FLOWER	ICE CREAM	CUSHION	BOOK
PUDDLE	TRUCK	DREAM	APPLE	RAINBOW
CHEESE	FOOTBALL	HAT	PENCIL	OSTRICH

MEMORY TEST

DO YOU HAVE A SIMILAR BRAIN TO YOUR BESTIE'S, OR ARE YOU SO DIFFERENT THAT YOU MAKE A PERFECT TEAM?

Without showing each other your results, swap places and try the other test. Write what you remember again. Now check your answers.

WHICH SMOOTHIE ARE YOU?

QUIZ YOUR BFFS TO FIND OUT WHICH SMOOTHIES SUIT THEIR
PERSONALITIES BY FOLLOWING THE FLOWCHART BELOW.

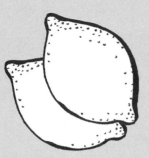

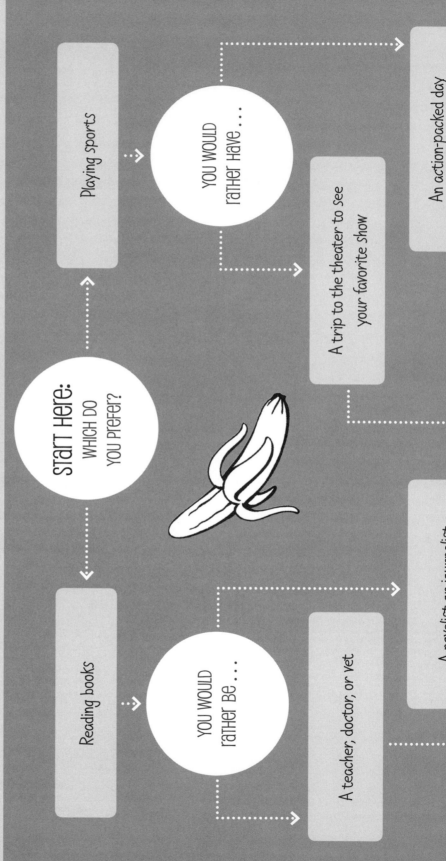

START HERE:
WHICH DO
YOU PREFER?

Playing sports

Reading books

YOU WOULD RATHER HAVE . . .

YOU WOULD RATHER BE . . .

A trip to the theater to see your favorite show

An action-packed day at a theme park

A teacher, doctor, or vet

A novelist or journalist

IN THE MORNING, DO YOU:

Put on your favorite music and get grooving?

Leap out of bed, ready to face the day?

Your smoothie is a **LEMON GINGER ZINGER**

You're bubbly, sporty, and always on the go!

AFTER SCHOOL, WOULD YOU:

Do your homework right away?

Finish your latest art project before doing your homework?

Your smoothie is a **TROPICAL MANGO PASSION**

You're a fun-loving and creative girl who's not afraid to try new things.

Your smoothie is a **BRAINY BANANA BLASTER**

Intelligent and studious, you love any brain-boosting challenge!

AT SCHOOL, DO YOU PREFER TO:

Sit at the back so you can help out your friends?

Sit at the front and try to answer all the questions?

Your smoothie is a **SWEET 'N' SOOTHING STRAWBERRY**

Kind and thoughtful, you're always there when your friends need you.

DESIGN a FORT

IN THE SPACE BELOW, WORK WITH YOUR BFF TO DESIGN
YOUR OWN SECRET HIDEOUT WHERE YOU CAN SPEND TIME
CHATTING OR CHILLING—NO GROWN-UPS ALLOWED! DRAW
ANY FURNITURE, DECORATIONS, AND ACCESSORIES YOU LIKE,
SUCH AS BEANBAGS, TWINKLE LIGHTS, OR STREAMERS.

Date .... Time .... Place ....

This page was completed by .... and ....

THE FUTURE'S IN YOUR HANDS

THE ART OF PALM-READING IS CALLED PALMISTRY. PRACTICED ALL OVER THE WORLD, IT IS SAID TO REVEAL A PERSON'S FUTURE AND SHOW THEIR TRUE PERSONALITY.

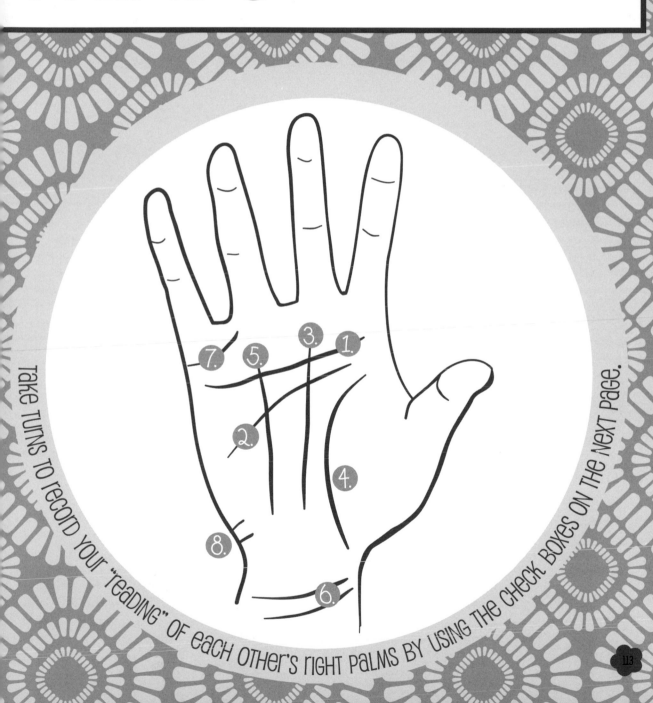

TAKE TURNS TO RECORD YOUR "READING" OF EACH OTHER'S RIGHT PALMS BY USING THE CHECK BOXES ON THE NEXT PAGE.

THE FUTURE'S IN YOUR HANDS

1. THE HEART LINE
Short: quiet and reserved
Long: outgoing and sociable

2. THE HEAD LINE
Curved: spontaneous and daring
Straight: practical and logical

3. THE FATE LINE
Faint or no line: easygoing
A clear line: ambitious

4. THE LIFE LINE
Long: bubbly and positive
Short: healthy
Faint: indecisive

5. THE SUN LINE
Short: future success
Long: wealth and happiness

6. THE LUCK LINE
Unbroken: 30 years of good luck
Gaps in the line: an exciting life with ups and downs

7. THE RELATIONSHIP LINE
Long and horizontal: you will have one long, happy relationship
More than one line: you will have more than one love in your life

8. TRAVEL LINES
One line: home-lover
More than one line: travel-lover

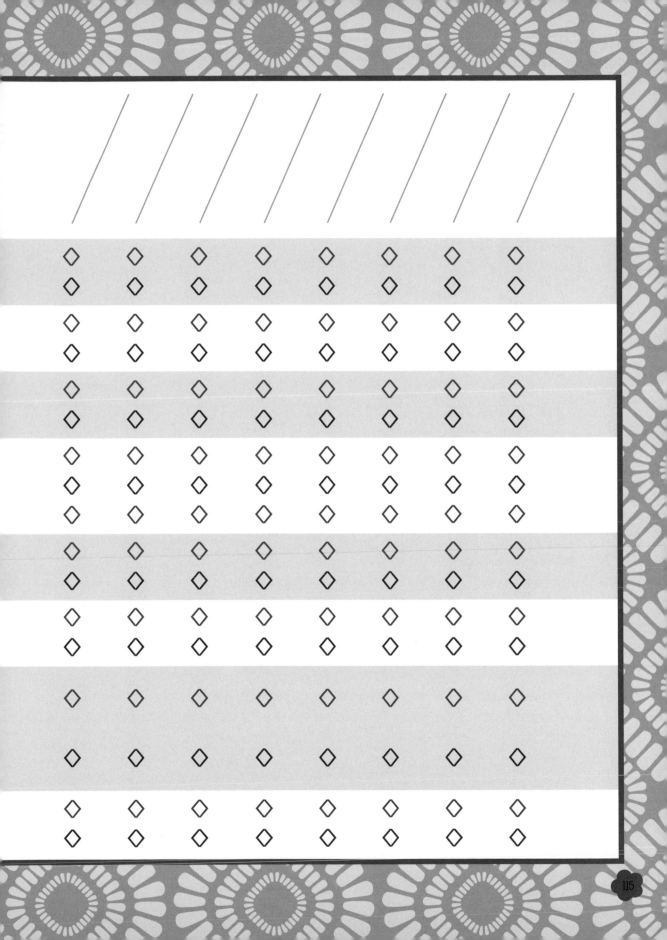

Bestie Band World Tour

All your besties in a band, traveling the world—what could be better? Fill in the boxes below with your BFF to put together your band and plan your world tour.

What would your band be called?

....

What kind of music would you play?

Rock ◇   Pop ◇   Hip-hop ◇   Funk ◇

What countries and cities would you visit on tour?

....

....

....

Date .... Time .... Place ....

Who would be in your band? (It doesn't matter if they don't play an instrument—anyone can take part in your bestie band!)

Lead singer ....

Lead guitarist ....

Bass guitarist ....

Drummer ....

Keyboards ....

Backing singer 1 ....

Backing singer 2 ....

Manager ....

What would be the name of your first hit single?

....

....

These pages were completed by .... and ....

BFF BOOK awards

LIST YOUR TOP FIVE BOOKS OF ALL TIME BELOW, STARTING WITH YOUR FAVORITE.

1. ....

2. ....

3. ....

4. ....

5. ....

Date .... Time .... Place ....
This page was completed by ....

GET YOUR BFF TO LIST HER FAVORITE BOOKS BELOW.

Compare your answers. Are there any titles you both love?
Circle them.

1. ....

2. ....

3. ....

4. ....

5. ....

Sometimes, two authors write a book together. If you
and your BFF wrote a book, what name would you use?

....

Date .... Time .... Place ....

This page was completed by ....

COLOR US HAPPY

This page was completed by ....

This page was completed by ....

GOING FOR GOLD

1

1. How long can you hold your breath?
Less than 10 seconds   ◇ 1 point
10-20 seconds   ◇ 2 points
More than 20 seconds   ◇ 3 points

2. How many times can you quickly say, "Kitty caught the kitten in the kitchen," without making a mistake?
Once   ◇ 1 point
Twice   ◇ 2 points
Three or more times   ◇ 3 points

3. In one minute, how many different words can you make from the word FRIEND?
One word   ◇ 1 point
Two words   ◇ 2 points
Three words or more   ◇ 3 points

4. How long can you look into a friend's eyes before you blink, laugh, or look away?
Less than 10 seconds   ◇ 1 point
10-20 seconds   ◇ 2 points
More than 20 seconds   ◇ 3 points

Total: ....

Date .... Time .... Place ....
This page was completed by ....

ask three friends to compete with you in the BFF olympics. Have each choose a competitor number, and write down who is which number below. Then, complete the challenges to reveal the winner.

1 .... 2 .... 3 .... 4 ....

1. How long can you hold your breath?
   Less than 10 seconds   ◇ 1 point
   10-20 seconds   ◇ 2 points
   More than 20 seconds   ◇ 3 points

2. How many times can you quickly say, "Kitty caught the kitten in the kitchen," without making a mistake?
   Once   ◇ 1 point
   Twice   ◇ 2 points
   Three or more times   ◇ 3 points

3. In one minute, how many different words can you make from the word FRIEND?
   One word   ◇ 1 point
   Two words   ◇ 2 points
   Three words or more   ◇ 3 points

4. How long can you look into a friend's eyes before you blink, laugh, or look away?
   Less than 10 seconds   ◇ 1 point
   10-20 seconds   ◇ 2 points
   More than 20 seconds   ◇ 3 points

Total: ....

2

Date .... Time .... Place ....

This page was completed by ....

3

1. How long can you hold your breath?
   Less than 10 seconds ◇ 1 point
   10-20 seconds ◇ 2 points
   More than 20 seconds ◇ 3 points

2. How many times can you quickly say, "Kitty caught the kitten in the kitchen," without making a mistake?
   Once ◇ 1 point
   Twice ◇ 2 points
   Three or more times ◇ 3 points

3. In one minute, how many different words can you make from the word FRIEND?
   One word ◇ 1 point
   Two words ◇ 2 points
   Three words or more ◇ 3 points

4. How long can you look into a friend's eyes before you blink, laugh, or look away?
   Less than 10 seconds ◇ 1 point
   10-20 seconds ◇ 2 points
   More than 20 seconds ◇ 3 points

Total: ....

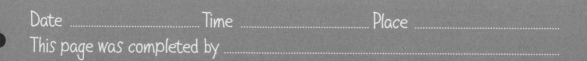

Date .... Time .... Place ....
This page was completed by ....

1. How long can you hold your breath?
   Less than 10 seconds   ◇ 1 point
   10-20 seconds   ◇ 2 points
   More than 20 seconds   ◇ 3 points

2. How many times can you quickly say, "Kitty caught the kitten in the kitchen," without making a mistake?
   Once   ◇ 1 point
   Twice   ◇ 2 points
   Three or more times   ◇ 3 points

3. In one minute, how many different words can you make from the word FRIEND?
   One word   ◇ 1 point
   Two words   ◇ 2 points
   Three words or more   ◇ 3 points

4. How long can you look into a friend's eyes before you blink, laugh, or look away?
   Less than 10 seconds   ◇ 1 point
   10-20 seconds   ◇ 2 points
   More than 20 seconds   ◇ 3 points

Total: ....

4

AND THE WINNER IS: ....

Date .... Time .... Place ....
This page was completed by ....

125

makeover mates

Stylist

....

Record the look here

Score

$\overline{10}$

My BFF's hairstyle:

Nail color/pattern:

Jewelry:

She looked awesome wearing:

She didn't look so good wearing:

Date .... Time .... Place ....

DRESS YOUR BFF UP IN THE CLOTHES AND ACCESSORIES SHE LOOKS GREAT IN AND DO HER HAIR AND MAKEUP. RECORD HOW FABULOUS SHE LOOKS ON PAGE 126. THEN ASK HER TO DRESS YOU UP AND FILL IN THE PAGE BELOW.

Stylist

....

Record the look here

Score

$\overline{10}$

My BFF's hairstyle:

Nail color/pattern:

Jewelry:

She looked awesome wearing:

She didn't look so good wearing:

Date .... Time .... Place ....

also available:

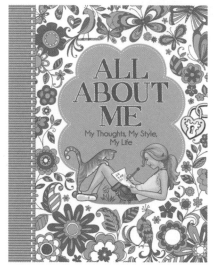

ALL ABOUT ME

BEING A GIRL

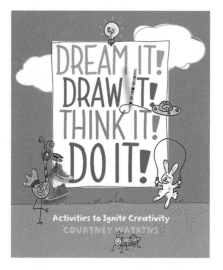

DREAM IT! DRAW IT! THINK IT! DO IT!

RAINY DAY UNICORN FUN